The State of Amerricuh

Written by

Mark Carter

Foreword

Looking at the advancements that have been accomplished during my short time here on earth, I've often times wondered if the past was even to be considered humane. What is it about the future generations that makes it to where the past has to wait on them before more advancements can be made in any given sector. At the same time, it appears as though the younger generations have to deal with a bit different approach to violence and violent crimes. I can't imagine being less than 10 years old and explaining a school shooting or murder suicide to an unknowing adult. Some come out of the grove saying, "It's time for a change America." Some come out saying, "We've got to go back to the church, they've got to put prayer back in school."

None of these 2 have ever officially left the parameters of most school campuses across America. Somethings we forget about like everybody isn't always on time and some kids have to deal with illnesses before being able to join their classmates.

In fact, on a larger note, a lot of adults deal with the same issues as well. The insurrection riots on the capital building are about as traumatic for most Americans as it is for a school shooting survivor. It only brought about a lot of harm to the same people they claimed they were defending. Now former President, Donald Trump has to deal with the advancement of felony sentences on the political battlefield. Time will tell where we stand as a whole. I've never understood the idea of attacking the innocent, but I'm as sure as the day is long that there are many regrets behind some of those actions. It happens to the best of us. We make an assumption and jump and forget we were unsure of where we would be landing.

I will be using a personal form of comedy throughout this book, but feel free to take in every word with seriousness of someone's last breath.

Joy to the World

"Hello World!! Here I am!!" I wonder if that's what

I sounded like while making my grand entrance into the world. It was probably more like the background of a horror movie. Can't remember the last time I heard someone say," I never cried, even when I was born"

That scenario would have been a hell of a mound of bragging rights, but I feel like there's a 100% chance that every baby cries at birth. It's a bit of a subliminal message that we come in to the world in that state of shock and the rest of the world is in the same state with us. "We were birth upon unity, but it was only to agree to disagree."

I also can attest to the fact that marriage comes with an automatic conversation about divorce. The divorce bug has no common enemy, it is literally a force to reckon with. I've seen the divorce bug run rampant in upper class and middle class, and be disappointed that lower class folks chose to be high school sweethearts and roommates rather than to opt into the inevitable conversation that some married people may even call tempting given the stress and time factors of the times. The funniest part of the process has to be the fact that it always seems like the couples you would expect to be divorced are actually the ones that stay together.

Within the first 5 years of entering life, I witnessed my

first terrorist attack. I believe the World Trade Center was attacked the first time in 1993. These were big ideas and actions for a child to take part in any kind of capacity. Could have been very easy to grow up overly patriotic or gear headed towards being brainwashed for the sake of warfare.

It was weird at times playing with a G.I. Joe playset, knowing that repercussions of those actions will always mean serious injury or even death. For some odd reason, a certain amount of conviction would come from time to time and I moved on to the hot wheel cars and video games. If I'm not mistaken, I also worked on a few cars to scale. These were pretty hard tasks for a child not yet in middle school yet, but everything worked out.

Carrying the Team

In the world of money, I believe the saying is," you could never have enough." I thought about arguing for a second but I didn't want to be the idiot that asked for less money. These are things that kids may argue about for weeks at a time. I'm sure some have never let some of their arguments go since their childhood, well into adulthood.

While in elementary
school I developed an affinity
for just about every sport that
I knew about at the time.
From soccer to basketball,
from baseball to football,
from wall ball and polo to
tennis. If there were rules and
physical activity, believe me
when I say I was front and
center.

The only bad part about
things like this is when
money isn't the issue, time
still is. In today's society we

are able to watch more sports based on the number of leagues and contrast there is available. I don't know if we would ever live to see a 4-sport professional athlete. It's just not possible. You've got to rest at some time. Being a child full of energy from an unknown realm, I would probably think the sensible me was flat out lying.

Entering adulthood, I realized how far away from some of those key principles and the discipline of these sports I had gotten. I had done all the stints of trying to go to the gym and trying to get so much cardio in every day. I finally had to accept the fact that it wasn't me getting lazy, it was just my body telling me it needed me to head in a different direction for a moment physically.

It's too easy to take up the, headstrong, push through the pain mentality. It takes discipline to know when to rest and how much rest you need. For some it could be their diet, and for others, it could be no more than the environment that surrounds them. I would grow up to notice these scenarios all too well.

Wayside not Bayside

I'm no Zach, as well as a Mr. Belding. Probably couldn't fill the role of Screech or Slater for that matter. I did however understand the roles of every individual and what happens in the midst of every social victory and defeat. Sometimes we may think that term, "I couldn't do anything about it," will set us free from ever down moment we may have about what happens to our peers, the adults that surround us, or even ourselves. Most people learn how to turn these moments into the catalyst for change that our country and the world needs.

Pressing ahead towards today's society, volunteer work has gotten more popular. Feeding the hungry and homeless is probably at an all-time high. These are all signs that as the human race we all know what to do. Why does it seem like those good deeds are what makes it seem to ignore what the problem really is.

We claim to be the strongest, most capable country in the world, but we are plagued with the same problems as the rest of the world. That's not in the aspect of trying to undermine the good intentions that well have, but only to identify the

very things that want to
defeat us.

Things happen to include
the subjects of poverty,
illiteracy, bankruptcy,
criminal background records,
fraud, acts of God, and I'm
sure the list could go on and
on.

One scene stands out to
me more than anything as far
as the chapter title is
concerned. Saved by the Bell
had many instances of
showing the village raises the

child mentality. From the relevance of the cafe to a real-life restaurant, down to the lectures the group would have to take on as a whole.

I would love to see the grown-up version of these same characters somehow. Not even just these, same from Family Matters and the other child sitcoms that we all witnessed in their prime.

Dangling in Adulthood

I frequently notice the
growing support and
protection it takes for adults
as well as children to survive.
The skepticism of helping a

stranger in a questionable neighborhood or road. The thought of a crime reoccurring again at your expense.

What will it take for some of the blunders of mankind to disappear? Will there truly be an Armageddon? Will we have to face God with our intentions with life carved with blood in our hands. How will we recollect our stances on authority in our lifetime?

Did we stand up soon enough,
or was it too little too late?

In Conclusion

The State of Amerricuh
isn't that bad, considering the
chances and opportunity we
have here. However, this isn't
reconcilable argumentative
creativity used to apologize
to the families of victims we

have seen perish over the last few decades.

We can't forget that as the population increases so does the chances of misfortune. Hopefully you have found the safety net in your" State of Amerricuh."

I would love to grant you a closed mouth and open ear. The due diligence report gives you all the information you need about your contributions to your society. Keep track of what you do and how you do it. The reward will forever remain in your heart.